P is for PUPPY: The A B C's of PUPPY

Positive, Proactive, Puppy Training

Written By Valeri Stallings

Photo by Taylor Stallings

15 Reasons why you should read, let alone purchase this book.

1) You just might screw your puppy up without it!
(Or vice versa).

2) I wrote this book for YOU.

3) It's a Dog gone good book.

4) This book will teach you how to effectively communicate with your pup in a fun positive way.

5) This book entails how to establish a relationship and a bond between you and your pup to enjoy for years to come.

6) I will teach you how to use hot dogs instead of harsh commands.

7) You will learn how to use an 'ice cream voice,' instead of an 'ice cold voice'. (No barking orders).

8) You won't need to use Ruff and Tuff techniques to train your pup.

9) This book will train you to be a Pawesome Pup Parent.

10) It includes cute puppy pics and houndish humor.

11) It's the Ultimutt book to last you decades. (Unless your pup eats it).

12) I give simple instructions with educated reasons behind them.

13) It is a fun and easy book. The most challenging word in here is homonym. :)

14) It offers troubleshooting guidance.

15) I can't be with you 24/7, but, for my students and my puppy book readers, I can offer helpful email and virtual tutorial assistance with your puppy rearing needs. Visit my website at SendRoverOnOver.com and search under 'PUPPIES' for instructions on how to connect with me via this route. This is a unique and convenient way to learn.

Table of Contents

Table of Contents cont.

Photo: Val posing proudly with Hooter, Lolli and Rolo. Rolo was my first and best business partner. He helped me temperament test over 1000 dogs.

Dedicated to Maggie.

My Chocolate lab. Maggie was Rolos mom.

It was Maggie that resulted in the worst days of my life. But she was also the initiation of this wonderful canine world I live in today.

Maggie was a fearful puppy. She became very aggressive with other dogs with time, age and very bad training methods. She caused me to lose my homeowners insurance, my relationship with my neighbors and my peace of mind. The traditional dominance based trainer I originally learned from with Maggie, taught me aversive training methods that maintained her fear, and enhanced her aggressive tendencies. This is one of the reasons I like the phrase "Question Authority." Maggie led me on a quest to discover a reason for her behavior, her aggression, and a treatment protocol. Her behavioral issues resulted in me seeking out answers deeper and deeper into the canine mind. This search introduced me to Positive Reinforcement methods of training and Behavior modification 15 years ago. This was the beautiful beginning of the second half of my life. I traded in 27 years of Nursing to become a Certified Pet Dog Trainer and a Behavior consultant. I am just short of my BS degree in Animal Science with a focus on Companion Canines. I provide behavioral consultations and training services to people and their dogs, and I am the founder of two of my communities first and best Doggie Daycares, Hotels and Training Centers, Send Rover on Over, INC. This is where I offer complimentary puppy social programs as a community service and help new puppy parents get off on the right paw.

Acknowledgements:

First and foremost my four daughters. These are the people I adore the most. They deserve to be acknowledged in a big way. They have endured quite a bit growing up with this dog mom. But, they have also been given the opportunity to see what happens when you follow your heart and learn where your passion can lead you.

Candice, the eldest, reminds me of me when I was 35. Only the better more durable, vibrant, skinny, full of life, intelligent, passion seeking, outspoken, hold the sugar coating version of me. She is a dog lover, but has a one eyed cat.

Jodi is the original co founder of my Business Send Rover On Over. She came up with the name that puts a smile on peoples face. Jodi is passionate about all living things on this planet. Including ants. She is the techno savvy one. The artist. She is an organizer and a problem solver. She is a Jack of all trades.

Shelbi, number 3 daughter became an experienced dog handler extraordinaire. She is also the decorator extension of my biz. Shelbi is a rescue dog mom, a major problem solver, a marathon crasher, lol, a philosopher and is acquiring her degree in Psychology.

Taylor has assumed role of SROO Business partner. She is the customer service specialist, marketing director, payroll advisor, resource person, up front person and behind the scenes person. She is also a dog handling expert. When Taylor was around 15 years old, she told me she thought it was a dumb idea to leave my $50 an hour nursing job for a silly dog business. Look at us now. :)

I need to thank my friends and the people that have encouraged and supported me in my decisions to take on a dog business and pursue a dog based career. Leaving a full time, 27 year, nursing job was scary to say the least.

Thank you to all the thousands of dogs and their people that have come in to my life, for over a decade now, seeking out assistance to better the quality of life and relationships with their dogs.

From repeat clients, to multiple generations of families.

To the hyper, difficult, stubborn, questionable, fearful, and challenging dogs that decided to eat some treats and get over it.

To the happy humans that clicked, treated, lured, participated, waited, and reaped the rewards of the relationship that came with training and learning how to communicate with their dogs.

To the people that looked at me as if I was a magician when I could get their dogs to perform, learn, change, evolve, pay attention or just plain ole lie down.

To every dog that catches my eye. And they all do.

And then there are my dogs. You will see their photos throughout.

Hooter, my yellow lab is the apple of my eye. Great story about Hooter is titled, 'Naughty puppy takes recreational class, turns hero'. That's a different book. Ha! Hooter and I are a team. He has taught me the more invested you are while working with your dog, the greater the dividend. He consumes my heart.

Piper is my feisty high energy American Eskimo. She was dumped in a park at 8 weeks of age with Parvo.

After 2 months of treatment and medical isolation, she bypassed her early social phase. She is living proof of how important the early socialization process is. Piper keeps up with Hooter and I, and keeps Hooter in check.

Piper has a fun enthusiastic spirit. She is a great athlete and is amusing to learn from because she demonstrates the learning theory of consequences and will give herself time outs.

Lolli was my little Papillion that died just this year. Lolli taught me not to underestimate the power of a three pound dog. She ran with the big dogs. Never needed a leash. Was an athlete runner, hiked 18 miles in one day, had 9 lives like a cat, and was a big little part of the pack.

About this book.

This book is meant to inspire, empower, and unleash your abilities to enable you to enjoy the puppy training process and allow it to be simple, positive, and light while having fun along the way. Puppy Training is a major part of the journey that leads you to adult dog contentment and proud parent bliss. When your dog is two years old, I want you to say, "I love my dog," with gratification.

What this book will teach you:

How to be Positive, Proactive, and Preventative.

This book will teach new puppy owners in simple terms how to communicate to your dog what you do and do not want them to do using positive reinforcement methods of training. While simultaneously reducing unwanted behaviors the nicest way possible.

Dog owners will learn how to communicate to their dog how to perform what are known as the basic manners. Basic manners for the purpose of this book will be sit, down, come, walk nicely, leave it, wait, mealtime manners, doorway manners, drop it and bring it. These basic training skills are taught in a simplistic form to get everyone kick started. Dog owners can expand on all these cues in another training class such as a Puppy All Star Class, Basic Manners class or a Canine Good Citizen class in the very near future. I like to recommend three class during the first year. A puppy class, a basic class and a fun class. One of my clients calls this getting multiple degrees. :)

The above basic manners will be taught using rewards, lures, happy voices, coaching, prompting and touch.

Using positive reinforcement techniques will make puppy training a pleasant experience and rewarding for both of you. Positive reinforcement methods of training is a bonding process for you and your new pup.

Positive reinforcement is a method of rewarding desirable behaviors. Behaviors that are rewarded in life will be repeated. It's a win win situation.

This book is also meant to enlighten you to the challenges that come with the doggie duties, obligations, and responsibilities of puppy parenting. Even though they may seem overwhelming right here and now, as the months pass by, so will your memories of shoe chewing, sock stealing, sleepless nights and cleaning chores and activities that are associated with puppy rearing.

Those days will soon be replaced with a happy adult companion canine to share tail wagging morning greetings, afternoon walks, and one-sided unbiased conversations into the sunset hours.

With proper care and training, your pup will soon be a your companion canine, family member, activity partner, exercise motivator, consultant, health coach, and the most wonderful four legged best friend with fur you can imagine.

Positive puppy parenting will get you off on the right paw to establishing communication techniques with your pup to last the life of your pup and for generations of dogs to come.

Positive reinforcement methods of training are historically, now, and futuristically, the best way to train. It is educated and scientifically based on how this system of learning works and why it's best for you and your dog.

Now I may be starting to ramble. Do you get the point? :)

Photo: Rexford yawning at my intro. :)

I will admit, I did write this book on a whim. After my wonderful

Puppy Coordinator retired, and I filled those shoes, I found a need to

put a book together quickly. Everyone learns differently and to be able to accommodate and enhance the learning process through literature for my puppy students, will be most beneficial in reinforcing the things we learn in Puppy class as well as top off anything we did not cover.

Thank you to those of you that invest the time and energy in a P+ socialization and learning program intended to help you learn, understand, and bond with your puppy in the best way possible.

Before the puppy comes home:

Some people put a great deal of thought into the puppy they acquire. For weeks, months, and sometimes years. For others, the puppy chooses you. Usually through a rescue or a spontaneous impulse buy at your local pet store.

Either way, the training aspects are the same. If from the breeder, the information directly below is for you. If you adopted the rescue pup or the Heinz 57, see breed specific behaviors and DNA testing to give you more insight to breed specific behaviors and behavioral needs.

How do you know you will be getting your pup from a good

breeder?

Photo: Patti the Breeder and 2 legged and 4 legged pups.

A good Breeder is a person that has passion for and is knowledgeable about the breed they are breeding.

They will be registered with a pedigree organization such as the AKC.

The mother dog of the pups should be limited to the number of litters she births.

You should be able to meet both the parents of the puppies and rest assured they are of good health and sound temperament.

The environment is clean and the puppies appear in good health.

They have been de-wormed and had their first round of vaccines.

They have been weaned and are eating solid food.

The best social condition for a puppy to be is inside the home with people and the family unit.

Exposure to children is a plus.

Some breeders will even initiate a puppy potty training process.

Photo: Caterina and puppies pile up in a play pen.

Things you should know before your puppy comes home.

Photo: Rich and J'Enelle and Finley. A bonding visit before the big

day.

The best time to bring your new bundle of fur home is at 8 weeks.

This allows for the puppy to have a good solid 8 weeks of Mother

dog/Puppy bonding. By this time they have been schooled and

disciplined in a natural way by their mom. Bite inhibition, canine communication, and play amongst its siblings are also the things puppies acquire and learn while cohabitating with their littermates.

Puppy training starts as soon as you get your pup home and the minute you walk through the door.

Having some ground rules and pre-established guidelines with everybody on board and in agreement will reduce conflict amongst household members and provide for continuity with training and a pawsative experience for your new pup.

When this new, happy, innocent, bundle of furry joy comes into your life, they come with a clean slate. From here on out is what they will learn primarily from you, and in your presence. The things that you teach, train, reward, reinforce, find cute and amusing, comical, influence, allow, discipline, disapprove of and do or do not manage will ultimuttly be the initiation of your puppies behaviors and on into adulthood. Other ways they learn will be from the consequences of their own actions.

You are now priming your puppy to furrever be the most wonderful, well mannered, affectionate, domesticated, companion adult dog that you could ever ask for.

It is much easier to prevent unwanted problems at this stage in the game then to try and modify them later when the behaviors may be engrained. (See 'Preventing unwanted behaviors').

Things you will need before the puppy comes home.

1) A Crate. Crates come in wire or plastic versions. For larger breeds of dogs, you can purchase a wire crate with a center divider panel that can fit your pup just right now, and the panel can be removed as he grows.

2) Baby gates. These are a lifesaver. Get a few. Place them at the tops and bottoms of stairs, in the front doorway, and definitely areas you would rather keep your pup out of for the mean time.

Photo: Baby gates and crates are a necessary safety item.

3) A comfy bed or blankets for the crate. Don't go all out on the price of your bedding materials. Some puppies will enjoy participating in bedding shredding adventures.

4) Feeding and drinking bowls. Ceramic and metal are best. Plastic can harbor germs and form ruff edges if your pup chews on it.

5) Toys. Toys serve a variety of purposes. Get a few different ones and see which ones your pup enjoys best. (See toys).

6) A collar. While there are lots of fashionable collars out there, I like the quicker release black buckle collar. If puppies or dogs become tangled during play, this type is easier to unbuckle verses the traditional buckle collar. Make sure it is a good fit. Too loose and it could be a tangle or choking hazard. Being able to slip 2 fingers in between the collar and your dog's neck is a good fit.

7) A leash. They come in 4 or 6 feet for the most part. A plain fabric lightweight leash is best.

8) A Name tag with the phone number engraved in BIG letters. A microchip is a great idea as well. Remember to activate it with the microchip company.

The First week:

Setting parameters.

Where will your puppy sleep? We all need to get some.

Where will your puppy eat? Attention all Chow hounds!

Where will your puppy potty? You gotta know where they gotta go!

Sleeping arrangements:

Photo: Rolo and Hug the Pug puppy sawing logs.

This is a personal preference issue. If your dog is a companion canine and considered a family member, then in the house will probably the choice for sleeping arrangement. Remember, this pup has just come from an everyday slumber party with lots of love and warm furry bodies to nestle up to. There will be an adjustment period. We cannot replicate their previous pup pack sleeping arrangements, but for them to know that someone is close by, and by using some tricks of the trade comforting products, will be a nice warm, and welcome start. I hope that it is no surprise to you that you will lose sleep. At least a few nights anyways. Establishing a comfortable routine will reduce the number of interrupted sleep time in the long run.

Crates are a great place for new puppies to sleep. This prevents wandering in the middle of the night and promotes the beginning of a crate potty training system.

Photo: Rudder pup and Wiley snuggling

Some folks opt for the puppy in their room, or in the kids' room or even in another room close by. Puppies seem to be more content and restful if they know they are nearby their new family members.

Photo: Hank and Jolene Snuggling. Crazy monkey and Stuffy dog are photo bombers.

Getting used to the new environment can take a few days. Some things that may help with the sleeping acclimation process is the location of the crate, the comfort level of the crate and bedding, and sometimes some white noise can be soothing. Things such as a clock, or a fan or even a TV or radio on low can calm a restless puppy at bedtime. Covering the crate with a blanket is often helpful as well.

Where and when your pup eats:

The most common places are in the crate and or in the kitchen, the laundry room or on surface areas that are easily cleanable. Puppies should eat a minimum of three times a day when they first come home. Ask your breeder which food product they were using and have it ready and at home when the new pup arrives. If you choose a different food, transition them over slowly.

Photo: Piper says the kitchen is the preferred place to eat in our house. We must have been celebrating, because we usually don't eat cheeseburgers.

Where to Potty:

When you gotta go you gotta go. My dog likes to Potty all the time! Outside is the preferred place for this process. Make sure the outside area is safe and supervised and free from anything that could make your dog sick. Take them out right when you get home and on a leash. They will probably do their business. Your job? Be ready! REWARD!!!! Remember, you have a clean slate. The behavior that is rewarded will become the desired or dominant behavior.

Other potty options are indoor turf boxes and puppy pee pads. On tile or easy to clean surfaces of course.

The First Year:

Photo: Val and super adorable lab pups at 6 weeks.

Doggie Developmental Stages:

Your pup will go through several developmental stages. Several of them have already occurred before you even met.

What are some important highlights about developmental stages and ages.

*Knowing the temperament of the puppy parents and that the gestational phase went well. (This is the stage in Utero).

*Socializing should happen before 12 weeks of age.

*Training should continue up until adulthood.

*Spaying or neutering is best at 6 months.

There are several stages of development that your puppy goes through in his lifetime. Having some basic knowledge of what they are and when they happen can help you to prepare, avoid and prevent. Things that happen during these phases can have a huge impact of the outcome of the temperament of your adult dog. Unpleasant occurrences that may happen during these stages may be modifiable later in life. But better avoidable if possible.

Prenatal: This is the period prior to birth. Traumatic events and temperament of the mother can be passed along to the puppies. A nervous Nellie Mommy can produce Paranoid Puppies.

Neonatal: This is birth to 2 weeks. They cannot see or hear yet. Exposure and gentle handling may be beneficial and produce more confidant puppies.

Transitional Phase: 2 to 3 weeks. This is a short period in which the eyes and ears open. Crawling, standing and walking occur. Solid food can be of interest and play fighting with littermates happens during this phase.

Socialization period: This time frame varies amongst individual puppies, but lasts from approximately 3 to 16 weeks of age. According to current recommendations that have been publicized over the past decade, this is the period of time that is most critical in social development, but quite often the most neglected. Reason being health and safety. It is quite often that new puppy owners are informed not to take their puppy anywhere until it is 16 weeks of age or fully vaccinated. The problem with this is that you bypass the critical and early social period. New puppy parents should be educated to safe socialization processes. This is the period of time when puppies should be introduced to as much new and novel stimuli that they can get their paws on. During the socialization period, is when they are known to be most receptive to new things. It may be difficult to introduce them to unfamiliar things and people after this point in time and have them respond in a friendly and confidant way. This is also when the first fear imprint phase occurs. (Please see Socialization).

Photo: Rocket demonstrating what a juvenile looks like.

Juvenile: 12 weeks to 6 months. Learning abilities are at their peak now. Continue to train your little sponges. The ability to socialize is on its way out and dogs become less tolerant of change. Sexual maturity usually occurs at just about 6 months. Time to spay or neuter. (See Spay and Neuter).

Photo: Handley celebrating 1 year.

Adult: 6 to 24 months of age. This is the point in time where they

are considered to have reached social maturity. Although this does range from individual dogs to individual breeds. They maintain

adulthood until signs of being a senior takes its role.

Senior: This is when they get their own AARP card in the mail.

Preventing unwanted behaviors:

Photo: Maggie Labradoodle impersonating a naughty

pirate pup.

You've heard the saying, "what you don't know, won't kill you,"

right? Well in this case, what you don't know, might hinder that loving feeling you are trying to establish with your pup. So lets read about this first.

Remember, your pup comes with a blank canvass. Lets paint the picture you will cherish for the lifetime of your dog.

Preventing undesirable behaviors can be done by knowing what those behaviors are, understanding why they do it, and preventing them from happening.

What might those undesirable behaviors be?

Here is a list of frequently mentioned undesirable behaviors that people would like keep out of the picture.

The Behavior   Why they do it   Preventing it

The Behavior	Why they do it	Preventing it
Barking	Dogs bark. This is the sound they make to communicate amongst each other. There are many reasons for barking. To alert or warn. To acquire or obtain something. To be let in or out of the house. In response to another dog. If they are startled. To get another dogs	Redirect your dog from undesirable types of barking. This means to call them away or divert their attention to something else. Yelling at your dog when they bark, is seen by them as, you barking with them. It's a bark fest! Instead, reward QUIET. Some dogs are more

	attention. To play. This could also be a way they communicate with you in an undesirable way depending upon how you respond to their barking.	prone to bark then other dogs. Some people choose dogs as pets keeping this characteristic in mind. One important thing to know is, if your dog looks at you and barks at you, and you think it's cute, and you respond in a reinforcing way? You have just reinforced barking.
Begging	To acquire something desirable from you. Usually food.	Never feed them from the table. Or from your meal. No matter how cute they look. It only takes ONE time to reinforce begging.
Biting	We will say puppy biting or nipping for this one. Puppies play and explore using their mouths and teeth.	Puppies will learn about a process called bite inhibition in puppy playgroups as well as from you. When puppies bite each other too hard, they stop play for a split second to let other puppies know "that hurt". If you 'yelp' like a puppy when your pup applies his teeth on you, he should interrupt play with you momentarily. Reward the break in

		play and offer a toy to chew on instead of your arm A good rule of thumb is no teeth on the skin.
Counter Surfing	They discovered goodies and treasures!	Keep counters clean and clear to avoid this in the beginning. Redirect and reward for 'leaving it'.
Destructive Behavior	Its fun! They are bored. They thought it was a toy. Teething. Separation anxiety.	Give them something to play with. Provide more exercise and stimulation. Participate in daily training activities.
Digging	It's fun! Burns off energy. Boredom.	More exercise. Provide them with a digging pit.
Escaping	In search of you. Separation anxiety. Boredom. Lack of exercise. Lack of human contact or bonding.	More exercise. Make sure the environment is safe from escaping. Do not isolate them much.
Grabitis	Not wanting to be escorted by their collars.	Avoid ruff collar grabs. Be gentle with collar escorts.
Growling	For a puppy, this should be vocalizing during play.	Some dogs are vocal. Reduce the stimulation.
Jumping	WINNER, WINNER,WINNER! The number one contender in undesirable behaviors. And the most preventable.	Your pup will most likely attempt to jump up on you at one point in time or another. As well as others. People's response to cute adorable puppies

	This behavior is exhibited in a desire to be closer to you.	is usually to pet them, right??? Well, this is the reinforcing force behind jumping. Please do not pet your pup for jumping from day one. Please teach all those involved the same rule.
Leash Reactivity	Usually bad experience on a leash or jerky tugging corrections.	Do not ever give leash corrections or tug on the leash.
Listening skill deficits	They are not motivated. Don't want to work for minimum wage. Scolding.	Make learning fun. Increase the value of the treats. Refrain from scolding your dog.
Potty in the no potty zone	They are not yet sure where to go.	Confirm that your potty training parties are on cue
Resource guarding	This is a natural way for dogs to retain resources.	Do not take valuables from your pup to show him who is boss. Reduce this with a give and take game

| Separation anxiety | Should be mild if at all at first after being removed from the original family unit. | Don't isolate your pup too much but also make sure you leave them alone for short increments so they understand you will return. |
| Zoomies or sudden bursts of energy | A sudden burst of energy that is short lived. | Encourage zoomies to be conducted outside. You can also turn the zoomie session into a game of fetch or activity time. Puppies and older dogs can get the zoomies too. |

Enough of the Doggy Downers. Back to more Puppy Uppers.

Here is a list of Alphabetized glossary of terms, training and general information for you to look up quickly.

A is for Alphabetized Puppy info

A is for Aggression:

Aggression with the tendency to hurt another dog person or puppy would be rare. I have met 3 pups in 10 years that I can safely call aggressive. One was a singlet in its litter. One was a possible drug ingestion exposure puppy and the other was a distemper survivor.

Consult your vet and a Certified Trainer with lots of puppy experience or a Behaviorist if you truly suspect aggression.

A is for Aversives:

An aversive is any consequence that follows a behavior that your pup finds unpleasant. Yelling "NO!" A shaker can, a squirt bottle, rolling your pup on his back, a choke or prong collar are all aversives.

I don't recommend aversives. But it is important for you to know why to not use them.

A) You can train your pup without them

B) They can make your pup fearful of you, aggressive, and or damage the bond and trust you are trying to establish with him.

B is for Behavior Modification:

Photo: Tucker about to learn about behavior modification.

This is one of the most important things you need to know in regards

to managing your pups undesirable behaviors. There will be times,

that training, ignoring, and redirecting is just not enough. You need

ammo. This is your go to tool. This is your back up plan. You need,

'Code Time Out'. This is the most constructive way to provide the lowest form of discipline in the nicest fashion that will make the biggest impact on your pup. It is called a time out. Also known as Negative Punishment. (Removing something to make a behavior decrease). Sounds mean, but it's not. Time outs need to be short and sweet and meaningful. Time outs need to be followed with acknowledgment of the alternative behavior. That means you give a treat NOW.

Example: Your pup is tugging on your skirt as you are getting ready for work. (For you gentleman, it's a kilt). You try to ignore your pups undesirable behavior, but you are afraid he will tear your favorite skirt with his jigsaw teeth. You offer a toy instead. Pup not interested. You ask for a sit or a down or a leave it. Pup not interested. You then would calmly escort your pup to a time out area for 3 seconds. (A time out area is in a pen, in a crate, outside a door, in another room).

Repeat….. THREE SECONDS!!!!! You then let him out. He will do one of two things. If he resorts to skirt munching, give another 3 second time out. If he looks at you with adoring puppy eyes as if to say, "Gee, what did you do that for? I was only playing?" Quickly give your pup a little piece of kibble, or a treat. Or some form of reward he considers more valuable then your skirt. He is now demonstrating a modified behavior.

If you have repeated the time out process 3 times, you both need a break. It is not a training moment, and your pup can go in their pen or their crate for a little while until you can work with them or supervise them. This process can be used for most undesirable behaviors. Try redirecting, training, and asking for alternative behaviors before applying Code Time Out.

B is for Bite inhibition:

One of the most important reasons to take your puppy to puppy play. This is the process of inhibiting your pups bite. In simple terms, teaching your puppy how to have a soft mouth. When puppies play with each other, they communicate what is too ruff. When your pup chews on you, you can 'YELP' in a similar fashion to another pup. You should then offer a more desirable toy then your arm. Some pups are relentless. You can offer them a little 3-second time out. Try to resume nice play without the piranha teeth on the skin. If they can play nicely, the reward is continued play. A little goodie as a reward also speeds up the learning process.

B is for Breed:

Photo: Designer breed foster puppy.

(That means Heinz 57).

Some folks take careful consideration and spend a good amount of

time researching their breed of choice. How much is that doggie in

the window? Pet shop puppy purchases often come as an impulse

purchase. So breed specific temperaments may not have been taken into consideration. Certain breeds behave in breed specific ways and have breed specific needs that need to be met. For example, Border collies do best when offered an outlet such as agility or herding. If these needs are not met, you could end up with some undesirable behaviors. Take into consideration your breed of choice and if it was a spontaneous decision, educate yourself to your dog breed specific needs. (See DNA testing).

C is for Crate Training:

If your puppy comes crate trained, you are miles ahead of the game. If you initiate crate training the first day he comes home, you are on top of it. If you start crate training a week after your pup is home, this could be a process. One of the biggest mistakes people make when crate training their pup is letting them out if and when they whine. So a little tuff love may be required here. Review the consequences as listed below. If you let your pup out of the crate when he whines, you have just taught your pup whining gets him out of the crate. You do need to make sure he is not whining to go potty. Crates are a great potty training tool as well as a safe place for your pup to sleep as well as a safe comfy place to play when you cannot supervise him directly at that time.

Crate Training 101: Most puppies will either come crate trained or easily become crate trained at this young of an age. The easiest way to crate train your pup is with a 9 day plan.

Have the crate in an area where your pup can frequent the crate, explore, climb into, have a meal, have a snack, rest, and play. So the crate is accessible to your pup ad lib.

Day 1, 2, and 3. Feed your pup all meals in the crate for 3 days with the crate door open.

Day 4, 5, and 6. Feed your pup in the crate all meals with the door closed but not latched.

Day 7, 8, and 9. Feed your pup in the crate with the door closed and latched.

Usually by this time, your pup will happily beat you to the crate awaiting good things to happen.

C is for Consequences:

These are either positive or negative events that happen to your pup depending upon what he has done to create a consequence to happen. Positive consequences result in the behaviors being repeated. Negative consequences result in the behaviors being avoided.

D is for DNA testing and breed acknowledgement:

Why your Mutts make up matters. Different breeds have different inherent health factors.

Different breeds respond to different training methods. I should say different levels of patience on your end. And you will learn what they may enjoy doing as a recreational sport if any. This will also help you to know what they were originally bred to do.

DNA testing can be done through your vet or you can send a saliva swab to DNA testing companies. The blood specimen is a little more accurate.

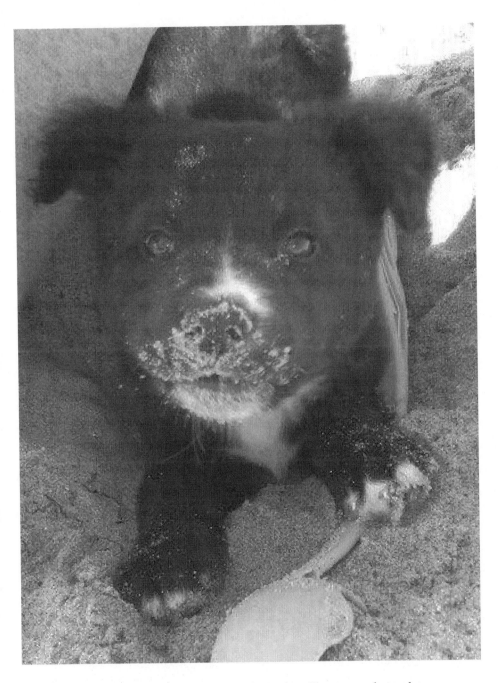

Photo: Meg is not the breed she looks to be. She was adopted as a

border collie mix. DNA tests reveal no Border Collie. Surprise!!!

D is for Dog Parks and Beaches:

Photo: Fe Fi Fo Fum. Jolene Sniffing the bench. What? A Beagle Sniffing? :)

Pros and Cons but not until 16 weeks. This is where the 16-week rule applies. Pros for the beach. The beach is a wonderful place for people and dogs. Tranquility for you and a wonderful water playground for your dog. Exercise, fun times, swimming and socializing are what your dog lives for. Cons to the beach. This is a common area for Parvo. And, under socialized dogs with too much freedom puts your dog at risk for altercations. Dog park Pros. Room to run and play and burn off energy in a fenced environment.

Socialize and make new doggy friends. Cons. Un-socialized dogs

with owners in hopes they will be social that day. Un-vaccinated

dogs. Uneducated people that don't understand play styles.

Photo: Hooter and piper happy as can be at the beach.

E is for Exercise:

Photo: Ryder making good use of his exercise ball.

Providing exercise for your pup in a safe area during the process pending full vaccinations and the ticket to exercise freedom, will need to be arranged in and around your home. Play groups with other pups can be arranged as long as the other puppy household is clean and safe from disease and has other nice puppy savvy dogs.

Look for clean and safe puppy play programs in your neighborhood to burn off a little extra energy in the interim.

E is for Exhaustion:

Photo: Rex pondering a nap.

This is YOU. You will probably be very tired during the first few weeks if not months. You need to understand, this puppy was a choice. He needs to be trained, entertained, fed, cleaned up after, and tucked in after a long day. The rewards will come sooner then you realize. Puppies are only puppies for less then a year. Hang in there.

F is for Feeding arrangements:

Where will your dog eat? Are their other dogs in the home? Are any of the dogs food aggressive? Will you free feed? Or provide specific times for feeding? These are some things to think about for that decision.

F is for Fearful puppy:

Puppies have personalities. I like to say they come in one of three different flavors. These personalities can change according to location and environment. The three flavors are

1) Shy and reserved,

2) Confidant,

And

3) Dominant, high energy and tarzanish.

These are my own personal categories and descriptions of puppies. Shy and reserved need lots of confidence boosting, nurturing, and protection from overwhelming events. They need more space. They are slow to warm.

The confidant dogs are even keeled. Happy, curious, busy, and social. Lucky dog parent you! Your job here is to help them maintain their status.

High energy, tarzan like play style, ruff and tumble and some times bullyish behavior goes here. Your job is intense. The work you need to put into your dog will result in a bond worth all efforts. You get to help your dog with impulse control and to bring it down a few notches. You may need to increase your caffeine intake while raising this pup.

You may want to consider a professional consultation with a good puppy trainer for a very shy or very dominant puppy very early on.

F is for Fleas and Ticks and Critters oh my!:

Photo: Paxton demonstrating the way he feels about fleas.

Did you know that 1 flea could bite your pup up to 400 times per day? Ouch! Bugs on your dog are nasty and so are the bug prevention products. Any way you look at it, products to prevent pests are called pesticides. You will want to do some research to determine which product works best for you, your dog and your lifestyle. There are topical products, ingestible products, and natural products available.

One of them should meet your personal pest control needs.

F is for Food, Feeding and Nutrition:

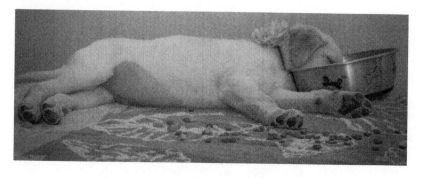

Photo: Adorable foster pup. Sometimes it's hard to decide between lunch and a nap.

New puppies should eat at least three times a day until they are about 6 months of age. Then there is the option of timed feedings as well as a free feeding program. One of my thoughts on a scheduled feeding program is it gives you leverage and conforms to a treat or food training program. I do not recommend any specific brands of food. There are foods made specifically for puppies and some foods that state they are for all life stages. You will want to choose what works for your personal lifestyle choices. I do like to educate people to the primary fundamentals of reading labels. The most important thing to know, is to provide the basic needs of the nutritional requirements for your puppy. The first five ingredients should be whole food products. The best food products can be purchased at most specialty pet food stores. And, I like to support small business owned pet stores. To avoid any intestinal incidents, it is recommended to start your pup on the breeders food product and transition over by mixing them half and half before feeding the new food entirely.

G is for Games and Tricks:

I am only going to review 1 here. It's cute and simple. Did you guess which trick it is? YES! It's shake! Or High Five. Maybe knuckle bump? Depends upon how cool of a dog parent you are. When your dog is in a nice calm sit, hold a treat in front of his nose and gently tap his Paw. Which one is up to you. If he lifts his paw off the ground or even loosens his stance on that paw, release the treat to him. Pair this action with your word of choice "shake," "gimme some," "high five," you get the drift. He will eventually start to offer his paw as a gesture for a goodie. And within time, merely for your warm adoring response.

Photo: Evo demonstrating shake.

Photo: Val gets excited easily.

G is for Grooming:

Photo: Scooter getting her first bath.

Advice from the groomer;

Your first grooming or bathing session can be conducted as young as 8 weeks. You can do this yourself, or find a positive reinforcement groomer that has a good reputation and is experienced with puppies. Depending upon the breed of puppy you have chosen, you may be forming a long relationship with your groomer as well.

The first bath should be nice and warm and comfy. If your pup is a little head shy, maybe even omit the face wash for the first few times. Check your puppies nails often. Puppy nails do grow fast.

You can even have your groomer teach you how to trim their nails.

Careful not to trim too short. If you touch their feet several times per

day and offer goodies at the same time, they should become

desensitized to having their feet and tushies touched.

Touch the feet…give a treat…Repeat…

Photo: Hannah and Evo and his first bath.

Holidays:

Photo: Odin is sporting a festive Santa hat.

Holidays come with Easter bunnies, Easter eggs and lots of chocolate goodies that are toxic to dogs. 4th of July comes with people, parties, and loud noises with bright flashing lights from fireworks. Halloween comes with lots of little strange looking people ringing the doorbell every 60 seconds.

Photo: Abbey and Santa Russ.

And Christmas comes with photos on strange, hairy, mens laps,

indoor trees with exciting shiny toys and tinsel, and all kinds of inviting extra curricular goodies that are only around one time of the year. Keep your pup safe from ingesting these items and exploring them with their mouths. For some pups, they take it all in. For others, is can be a major anxiety inducing event. Desensitizing your pup on a gradual basis and heavily rewarding bravery is the best way to approach fearful behaviors. (Consult a Behavior Consultant if these fears seem extreme and you are not able to help your pup overcome them).

Ice Cream Voice:

This is your happy training voice. Who can say 'Ice cream' without a little joy in their voice? This is a high-pitched, happy voice, that gets your pups attention. Happy voices also promote happy hormones to be transmitted in the brain. You can easily train your dog with a normal tone of voice. Save the emergency voice for emergencies! Barking orders is not necessary. :)

Leashes Harnesses and Tools of the trade:

Leashes should be four two six feet in length and a lightweight fabric. Harnesses are great for all dogs to walk in, or just to make a fashion statement. Some harnesses actually create the desire for some breeds to pull. Early leash walking exercises will promote nice leash walking. But in the event your pup grows fast and is on a mission to get somewhere, get a no pull front buckle harness. (Never use a choke chain, prong collar or shock collar on your pup).

M is for Meet the Family:

Everyone wants to meet the new puppy. Pizza party time!!! Bring it on!!! Parents, In laws, Aunts, Uncles, Cousins, Children, other dogs in the fam. Start introducing everyone early and often.

Photo: Chopper demonstrating wonderful big brother skills to Rex.

How to introduce the new rover to the old rover. Depending upon the temperament of your old dog, as well as the new pup, will determine the ease of this transition. Take it slow. Keep it positive. Put the pup in a crate or a pen and let your old rover sniff around and reward him with some high value goodies. He will think that this new puppy makes chicken fall from the sky. Get it!

Photo: Wiley meets Zipper

Always supervise these two until you are 100% sure all is right in the world of siblinghood. Do not scold your old rover for growling at the new pup. This is how they communicate. This is how adult dogs school puppies. This is a part of the communication process between the old rover and the young rover.

If this transition is challenging, consult your trainer.

Photo: Introducing Handley to Rex. Keeping it happy.

N is for name:

Photo: This is Finley. Great name, right?

What shall we name the puppy? You can come up with potential names before the puppy comes home, but sometimes the personality your pup arrives with, can spark an idea for a great name.

Dogs respond well to single and double syllable names. Abbey, Piper, Hooter, Lolli, Rolo, Rex and Finley are great dogs names. (Those are some of my dogs names so I'm a little partial).

Super long names are great for the AKC records.

Someone on YouTube did name their dog, 'Cheeseburger Machine Gun Chuck Norris'. Say that 10 times at the dog park. I don't recommend you name your dog 'FIRE'!!!! (Hopefully for obvious reasons).

Bella, Stella, Mac and Max seemed to be the most popular names for 2014. One of my daughters has a Pickles and a Lunchbox. These names always get a smile especially from children, as well as the general public.

Finding the meaning of a dogs name in a different language is a fun popular way to go as well.

Naming your dog can also relay an image. You may not want to name your dog 'Killer' if he is a therapy dog.

N is for Never:

I don't want to interrupt all the fun and furry content of P+.

I am not going to spend time informing you of what traditional or other methods of training consist of, but here is a brief list of things to avoid so not to confuse or damage the relationship or bond you are trying to have with your dog.

Lets Nip it in the bud.......

Do Not:	Why Not:
Use a choke collar, prong collar or shock collar on your dog or puppy.	They can hurt your puppy and cause behavior problems and they don't teach your pup what you do want them to learn.
Do not rub your pups nose in urine or feces.	This does not teach them where to go. It teaches them to be leery and afraid.
Never alpha roll, dominate, ear pinch or spank, smack, flick or flail at your puppy.	These are abusive maneuvers. Painful punishment is never necessary when attempting to teach any living thing
Do not spank your pup with newspapers or anything.	This makes them fearful and they come become neurotic over certain items.
Do not kick your pup or knee them in the chest if they jump up.	This is a painful technique that may teach them to be afraid to come close to you.
Do not pinch your pups toes or step on their feet if they jump up.	Same as above.
Do not introduce puppies to other puppies or dogs on a tight leash unless the leash is very very loose or preferably dropped and the dogs seem very friendly and receptive to an introduction.	This is not a natural way to introduce dogs. It may start a dog fight and your pup may become reactive on a leash if he has a bad experience.

Do not tug on, jerk, or give your pup corrections when you are out for a walk.	These tugs may cause your pup to negatively associate towards people and other dogs and may cause fear and or aggression.
Do not yell at your pup if they bark.	When you bark orders, you are promoting a pack bark session.
Do not allow your pups to fence fight or be harassed by neighboring dogs.	This can cause unnecessary stress in your pups life and may generalize over into other areas
Do not allow your pups to access poison or plants or things that could make them sick	Puppies explore with their mouths and this could result in a vet visit.
Do not yell at your pup to scold him.	Yelling can instill fear and damage your relationship. Why are you yelling at your pup anyway? Did you leave something out? Was he not properly supervised?
Do not encourage unwanted behaviors.	Barking, Jumping, Begging, Escaping, Biting, etc.
Do not take food or bones or other items from your dog to show him who is boss.	Your dog may become a resource guarder.
Do not use a harsh voice when training.	A normal or happy voice works best. Save loud or firm voices for emergencies.

P is for Positive:

What is P+ training? Rewarding your dog for desirable behaviors. Adding something rewarding to strengthen behaviors. Positive means to add something. What is rewarded, becomes a dominant and desirable behavior.

Photo: Riley. Happiest Keeshond puppy ever.

P is for Potty Arrangements:

Gotta have one. Showing your pup where his new potty party will be held, can be step number one, right when you get him to his new home. Options for potty places are the back yard, on a potty pad in a special room, a special litter box, or indoor sod box specifically designed for dogs.

Take your pup to their desired potty location. When and if they do their business, have a potty party!!! Give them a little goodie. Take your pup or show them their spot every two hours in the beginning. Reward for proper potty usage. In the event you take your pup to the potty spot, and they do not go. Put them in the crate for another hour and try again then.

Photo: Rugar says the grass is his fave place to potty.

Allowing your pup full roam of the house is setting a course for disaster. If he potties without your knowledge, that may very well become his new favorite spot to go. Not a fun party. Potty training will need to start from scratch now. Never rub your pups nose in poo or pee. This creates confusion and will cause him to be afraid of you. If you catch him, you can gently startle him and escort Spot to the correct spot. Hence the recommendation for constant supervision. Your pup will give you indicators that they need to go. Sniffing in circles is a good one. Whining for no apparent reason. Wanting to go out or in the direction of the rewarded potty party spot is another. I'm a doggie door fan. You can also purchase cute little potty bells that you can teach your pup to ring when they need to do their business too. It should come with instructions.

P is for Preventative:

All those things we don't want our pups to do when they are adults, starts here and now. (See Preventing unwanted behaviors).

Photo: Lucy and Sophie impersonating bad girls

P is for Proactive:

Making things happen and preparing for the future. Teaching the skills you want your pup to learn and know as an adult, NOW. Understanding how your pup learns by reading this book and participating in puppy school. Taking a proactive stance towards preventing unwanted behaviors in the future, by not reinforcing them NOW. These are all proactive measures.

P is for Puppy Proofing your home:

Having a puppy is like having a new baby in the home. We need to puppy proof it. Anything at your puppies level that he has access to will be inspected by his mouth. Children's toys are not differentiated from puppy toys. Shoes as other personal items left out or on the floor are fair game for puppy teeth inspections. Furniture may be chewed and rugs may be pawed at. Carpeted areas are a source for puppy accidents that are difficult to clean and a media for flea infestations. Baby gates are great. So are tile floors. Puppy pens are nice and simulate a playpen for a toddler.

Redirecting:

This is the process of asking your dog to do something else other then what he is doing that you don't want him to do. Requesting an alternative behavior. Your dog does not understand "stop that!" Redirecting is saying "don't do that, do this please".

Photo: Rocky taking a break for a photo op while discovering the

yard.

Resource guarding:

This is where your dog may growl or fight over food, toys, treats, his bed etc. This is a natural behavior that comes with survival instincts. This is a behavior that will allow your dog to maintain resources that he feels belong to him. Trading his resources for high value treats will reduce his fear of loosing things he feels are important to him. Taking his resources from him to show him 'who is boss,' can result in aggression. (Consult a trainer or behaviorist).

S is for Socializing:

Do it early. Do it safe. Kids. Dogs. People. ETC.

This is one of the most important things you can do with your pup. I have unfortunately heard this phrase too many times. "DO NOT TAKE YOUR PUPPY ANYWHERE UNTIL THEY HAVE HAD ALL THEIR SHOTS." This is the worst advice any puppy parent can hear. On the contrary. You need to "TAKE YOUR PUPPY EVERYWHERE WITH YOU." As long as you are able to carry them, stroll them, drive them, push them, or pull them. They need to see things, hear things, smell things and become familiar with all things in the world that will be in the presence of in their life.

Photo: Happy Social Pups at puppy play.

Photo: All the puppy play pics are fuzzy with lots of motion from

busy happy pups.

Socialization checklist:

Airplanes___	Helicopters___	Rain___ Hail___ Thunder Snow___
Animals___ Cats___ Ducks/Birds___ Rabbits___ Livestock___ Horses___	___ Lawnmowers___	Sirens___
**Children___	**Men	Smells_____
Clapping___	Motor Cycles___	Wagons___ Strollers___
Car washes___	People with canes or walking sticks__	Trash Trucks___
Cheering___	***People in Uniform___ ***People in hats___	Vacuums___
Construction___	People with umbrellas___	***Veterinarians___ ___

**Different ethnicities___	People Dancing___	Waterscapes___ Beach___ A Pool___
Drive thru's___	People with beards and facial hair___	Women___
Elderly People___	People that walk funny___	Free lance boxes _____
**Fireworks___	Stairs___ Automatic doors___	_____

Hair dryers_____	***Skaters___ ***Skateboards___ ***Bikes	_____

Check these items off as your pup encounters them during their first 16 weeks. Socializing is more then meeting one or two dogs or people. It's exposing your dogs to as many sights and sounds and novel stimuli that you would like him to feel comfortable around. Pay special attention to areas that he will need extra exposure. For example, if you are a preschool teacher, exposure to children would be a high priority. Trial exposures also evaluates how well he will respond to these new experiences.

The boxes with an asterisk are things that are a more common concern for pups as reported by their people.

(See Fearful Puppy).

Photo: Rex meets the phone repairperson.

S is for Supervising:

Photo: Rex finds a quiet nap spot under the dryer.

Know where your puppy is at all times! Unsupervised puppies get into trouble, danger, and potty where they should not. When you cannot attentively supervise your pup, he should be in a crate or playpen.

S is for School:

Photo: Ruby graduating from Basic manners.

Puppy Kindergarten. Puppy All Star. Basic Manners. Canine Good Citizen. How Mensa will your puppy be? Don't forget the extra curricular activities! Agility. Scent Tracking. Flyball. Dock Jumping. Hiking. What else? Get out and play with your dog.

Photo: Hooter loves Swimming and Dock jumping classes

Photo: Hooter on the Wave Runner.

Photo: Piper waits her turn for a ride.

Photo: Piper coming out of the agility chute.

S is for Spaying and Neutering:

This should happen around six months of age. This does vary according to current breed standards, breeder contracts, and vet recommendations. Puppies from shelters or rescues will usually be spayed or neutered upon adoption. This process is important for avoiding unwanted puppies in this community. It can also reduce some unwanted behaviors. Please! Please! Please! Do not state you do not want to alter your pup to have a litter of pups. Leave that to the professional breeders. There are lots of nice dogs in shelters that are without a home.

T is for Teething:

Your pup will start to loose their puppy teeth around 3 to 6 months. Baby teeth in your pups mouth are pushing through their gums making room for bigger teeth. This can't feel good. But chewing on things does. Have plenty of teething relief chew objects available for this phase. Giant frozen carrots are good, as are chicken broth dipped and frozen rope toys. There are specifically made freezer toys as well.

Photo: Evo demonstrating chewing on a nice rope toy.

T is for Toys:

Dogs need toys. There are a variety of toys that serve a variety of different purposes. Teething toys, exercise toys, interactive toys, bonding toys, cuddling toys and learning toys. Rope toys are good for individual play, teething and interacting with other dogs and pups. Squeaker toys are entertaining because, they squeak! Balls are interactive toys in which you and your pup and your family can teach a round of fetch. Good for exercise, bring it, and drop it skills. Frisbees are a sport toy and an outlet for certain breeds of dogs. Soft stuffed toys often get shredded. This is what dogs do. Buy cheap ones if this is concerning to you and make sure they don't ingest the squeaker or fluff. Kongs and rubber toys are close to indestructible, and when stuffed right, can provide up to an hour of solo entertainment in the crate. Feeding balls, cubes, and jugs are available as toys to reduce boredom and destructive behavior. And, there are several lines of genius toys out to help you expand your dog's brainpower. Super cool toys to develop super cool dogs. Try to limit the toys you have out for your pup to play with to only a few toys at a time. Rotate your toys and maintain their newness and novelty. A word of advice, a toy shoe is hard to differentiate between your favorite stiletto. Get it? Got it? Good.

Photo: Gunther and his Soft stuffed mini me.

There's too much room on this page, so I will tell a little story about little Lolli. Lolli was purchased by an individual from an out of state breeder at the age of 5 months. Lolli was just under 3 lbs at her time of arrival. Papillions are of sweet and smart temperament. But not Lolli.

Photo: Lolli and her squeeky toy woke us up every morning.

She was very timid and would not come out of the corner. Her adoptee described her as disrupting her houshold of four other dogs and she needed to go SOMEWHERE! ANYWHERE! And Now! I took her temporarily. I fell in love with her and turned her into a lab.

Lol. She lived with me happily ever after. The End.

Photo: Handley and his Birthday Loofa

Photo: Franni Lee posing with some favorite toys.

T is for Trainer:

Photo: Val and Kate and Beau graduating from Pup S.T.A.R.

How to pick the best trainer. Right up there with choosing the Vet and the Groomer. Dog training has become a profession. A professional dog trainer will belong to professional organizations and have some form of education under their belt. Certified pet dog trainers use positive reinforcement methods of training. The APDT has a website and a trainer search tool for areas all over the US. Ask your friends and Family and Vet who they like. Questions to ask a potential trainer. 1) Are you certified? 2) How did you acquire your education to be able to train people and dogs? 3) How many years of experience do they have?

4) How many puppies and their parents have they provided services for? 5) Do they have references? 6) What kinds of tools do they use for training?

7) For Walking? 8) For Behavior Management?

Avoid trainers that use aversive tools such as choke, prong, and shock collars. Shaker cans and dominance techniques and yelling "NO" are a no.

Treats:

Things you need to train with. A primary reinforcer. A reward. A motivator. Goodies. Something yummy and valuable. Worth working for. The value of the treat is determined by your dog. Most pups won't work for a piece of kibble in a group class. But they may not take their eyes off you for a pea size piece of white meat chicken. I tell my students to bring something moist and greasy that you can't just put in your pocket. (Hence the treat training pouch).

You should get a happy, tail wagging, pupil dilating, emotional response from your dog when you offer him a treat. If he does not respond to what you are using, you may need to offer him a wage increase. For example, kibble = minimum wage and chicken = premium pay. "I'm working hard, can I get a raise please?"

Photo: Piper demonstrating a polite way to ask for a raise.

V is for Veterinarian:

How to choose your vet.

This will be a very special person aiding in the decision making process of your pups health and well being, in sickness and emergencies. Into adulthood, and on and up and into the golden geriatric years. This is a relationship.

Most puppy books and puppy informative websites will advise you to consult with family, friends, and acquaintances on their vet choices. Finding a vet with similar philosophies behind pet care can help you make decisions as well.

My biased but educated opinion is to inquire into what your vet's stance is on early, safe, and educated puppy social programs. A vet in support of a safe puppy social program, is likely to be current on not only your puppies overall health knowledge, but their behavioral health as well. A vet in support of puppy social programs is also more likely to be current and up to date on medical and behavioral health trends that you and your puppy will benefit from. One thing that I personally look for in a vet, is the ability to offer choices and rationale with valid explanations for why a treatment, surgery or medicine may be recommended. This probably comes from 27 years as a Registered Nurse.

Here are some other things to help you make a decision.

Good communications skills. Compassionate, professional, knowledgeable and skilled vet techs and office staff.

Vet techs are conducting a good portion of the handling interventions with your pup. Vital signs, touching, assessing, and vaccinations are given by techs. Are they proficient and competent as well and caring and compassionate? For both you and your pups needs?

Is the office clean? Does it smell fresh? Do they provide educational materials in the lobby? What about social media or facebook. Do they have email options?

Are the credentials of the staff available for you to review? Are they members of a professional organization? What about follow-ups? Phone calls and sympathy cards say 'we care'.

Another word of advice for you and your pup. ADVOCATE. Be informed. Get second opinions. Do research to confirm and validate you are making the best decisions available for your pup.

Vaccines:

Photo: Bailey Lynn says, "don't debate, vaccinate!"

These are the recommended guidelines for puppies in CA.

Depending upon your demographic location, your vet may

recommend some additional vaccines according to the diseases that

may be prevalent in your community.

Why do we give it and what does it prevent.

**Rabies Causes Madness and convulsions. Fatal.	At or just under 16 weeks. Boosters annually then every 3 years
**Distemper	At or just under 16 weeks.

Causes A multi system viral disease.	Boosters annually then every 3 years
**Parvovirus A contagious virus that causes internal bleeding.	At least 3 doses between 6 and 16 weeks of age.
**Adenovirus A respiratory disease	At least 3 doses between 6 and 16 weeks of age.
Para-influenza An infectious respiratory disease	First dose 6 to 8 weeks then every 3 to 4 weeks until 12 to 14 weeks old.
Bordatella A contagious respiratory disease	1 dose of intranasal or 2 doses of injections. 6-month boosters recommended for pups that participate in dog parks, daycares, and boarding.
Lyme disease Tick transmitted disease that affects the joints	1 dose at 9 weeks with the second dose 2 to 4 weeks later

Leptospirosis A bacterial disease that causes flu like symptoms	First dose at 12 weeks and the second dose 4 weeks later
Canine Influenza Another type of respiratory disease	First dose 6 to 8 weeks. Second dose 2 to 4 weeks later.

The Vaccines listed with the ** are considered core vaccines. Core vaccines are recommended for all puppies and non-core vaccines are advised according to your pups lifestyle.

These are the initial vaccines that your pup will need to get him off to a healthy start. Your vet will inform you of when your boosters are required following the initial doses.

The Bare Bone Basics of Training your Pup:

Positive Reinforcement methods of training is in my opinion the best method of establishing communication skills with your dog in a fun, rewarding, compassionate way that helps you build and establish lifelong habits and a solid bond with your canine companion.

How does your Pup learn?

Photo: Chevy displaying his genius look

Puppies and all living things learn two ways primarily.

Through Association also known as Classical Conditioning

And

Through Consequences that occur to your pup also known as Operant Conditioning.

I will try and keep this part as simplistic as possible.

Classical conditioning:

Your pup will learn to think. "Aha! THIS makes THIS happen".

This is where your pup associates SOMETHING with ANOTHER THING.

Either a negative or positive thing.

Example:

Positive Associations;

When mom gets the leash, we go for a walk. The pup is associating the leash with a walk. Usually a pleasant thing. So they are learning or associating that leashes represent things that are pleasant.

The flip side of the coin.

Or,

Negative associations;

When I opened my dog daycare business, I lost some of my domestic skills. No great loss. When I would bake, the smoke alarm in the living room would usually be triggered. My Smart Chocolate lab Rolo, soon associated the oven door thing, with the sound of the smoke alarm thing, beeping, and he would exit the building as soon as he heard the squeak of the oven door opening. He formed a negative association to the sound of the oven door. It was scary for him.

Can you think of a Positive Association your pup has or will learn?_____

_____

How about a Negative

one_____

_____

Operant Conditioning:

This is where your pup will think, "Aha! When I do THIS, THIS happens." Your pup learns about positive and negative consequences.

Positive consequences;

You are sitting at your desk and your pup walks up and nudges your hand. You look down at him adoringly and pet him. He has just learned that the consequences of nudging your hand gets affection or attention.

Rewards are the consequences of nudging in this case.

Negative consequences;

These happen in everyday life by the way, and or they can be staged.

Your dog chases a cat, the cat turns and swats him. This should teach

him not to chase cats due to the unpleasant consequences involved.

Photo: Rudder learning consequences. When the cat says "no," he means "no."

Can you describe what a Positive learning event may be?

_____

_____

How about a Negative one?

_____

_____

OK, your pup already knows how to sit, or put their fanny on the ground, right? They lie down to relax, they come to you when invited, (for now), and they will follow you a little bit when prompted.

But,

they do not yet know the English words that pair with the above actions, right? Sit, down, walk, come, stay, wait, etc.

That's what we will learn now. How to teach our pups the English words that goes with sit or bottom on the ground etc.

Get ready to set yourself and your pup up to succeed.

Make it simple.

Keep it short and sweet. 1 to 3, 5 to 15 minute sessions per day.

Recognize your dogs drive to learn.

Keep going.

Recognize when your dog is 'over it.' :)

Call it a day. End on a happy note.

The Name Game:

The name game, is also known as a focus exercise or 'look at me.' It is acquiring eye contact. Getting your dog to look up at you. It's not come, and it's not sit. It is "Look at my eyes please." Hocus pocus focus on me. This game also strengthens your dogs response to his name. Say your dogs name with a happy voice. One time. (See Ice Cream Voice).

Val drags a treat to her eyes to get Hoover to make eye contact. The second he looks at her in the eye, she says his name, "Hoover", and gives the treat. Start saying your dogs name and right when he looks

at you in the eye…. Give the treat.

Stand up nice and straight and tall. (Or sit :))

Say your dogs name one time in a nice happy voice.

Right when he looks up into your eyes quickly offer a treat and say

"Good Job."

Repeat this exercise until your pup has this down pat.

Smoothing out the Ruff Spots:

Dog won't make eye contact.

Drag a treat from in front of your dogs nose and up to your eyes.

Right when he makes eye contact, or looks in that direction, say,

"YES," and quickly offer the treat.

Attempt to say your dogs name after a few sessions without holding

a treat over your eyes.

Right when he makes eyes contact, let him know, "YES! Look at

me! Thata boy/girl!"

Avoid having the treat in plain site where your dog can be distracted

by it and want to look at the treat instead.

If you do not use a treat pouch, you can put the treat behind your back. Or, you can use a treat pouch.

Sit:

Sit Happens.

How to teach your dog to sit.

Photo: Dave and Hoover demonstrating the Hillbilly version of sit.

This is the second easiest thing to ask of your dog.

Hold a treat in front of your dogs nose.

Be patient.

Wait for it.......When their bottom hits the ground, release the treat.

Viola!

Do this several times. When they start to get the hang of it, pair it with the word "SIT" with the action of their bottom sitting on the ground.

This process is called 'LURING'. To entice, lure, attract, tempt, allure, lead.

Smoothing out the Ruff Spots:

Your Dog Doesn't Know Sit.

Why won't your dog sit?

Assess surface area. Is it cold? Is it foreign? Is it scary? Is it uncomfortable in some way for your dog? Try a new spot. Try having them sit on a blanket or a towel or a bed or a couch. Is this starting to sound Dr. Seus-ish?

Is your dog jumping up to get the treat?

The treat is held too high for them to sit or you may be moving your treat up and down or all around.

Keep your hand still at the level of their nose while they would be in a sit position.

Try a technique called "Capturing." This is where you catch the dog in a sit position and say, "SIT," and quickly reward. Sit Happens right?

DO NOT push on your dogs bottom to get them in a sit. This stimulates their 'Oppositional Reflex'. A reflex that responds in the opposite direction of what you actually want them to do. Usually pushing on their hindquarters will prompt them to stand or be suspicious of just what you are doing back there.

Down:

Or Lie Down. By the way, the word 'DOWN' should be used for lie down. And the word 'OFF' used for get off of things. Your pup does not know homonyms. (2 meanings for one word). It's best to start this cue from a sit position. When your dog is in the Sit, take your food lure, hold it in front of their nose, and slowly lower the food to the ground in front of your dogs front paws. When they offer a Down position, quickly reward them with the treat. After several sessions of luring into a Down, start to pair the word DOWN, as we did with Sit. If the butt pops up? Start all over.

If your dog is close, then release the treat at three quarters of the way down and start using a technique called 'SHAPING'. Shaping is rewarding approximations of behaviors offered while getting closer to your ultimut goal.

Start in a sit position

Take the treat in front of his nose and slowly lower

your hand to the ground right in front of him.

When he assumes the down position, release the treat!!!

Smoothing out the Ruff spots:

Down can be challenging for extra large and extra small dogs. This is from my experience.

XL dogs seem to take a little more time to get down there. Be patient.

XS dogs seem to like different surface material that is a little on the comfy side. A blanket or bedding. A towel or a bed or couch for a surface.

You can also train your dog the down using the capturing technique as with the sit.

Please do not pull your dogs front legs down or attempt to push your dog into a down. This will once again prompt a response from their oppositional reflex.

Stay and or Wait:

These terms can be used interchangeably.

I have heard trainers in the past say Stay is for a good amount of time and Wait is just for a second or two. You can choose.

One interesting story I would tell in my classes was that of an Advanced Obedience Class. They would place their dogs in a Sit Stay on top of a mountain and all drive away in separate cars, to come back to their Rovers still in an amazing Sit Stay. Impressive.

I am more in tune with teaching the basics, communication skills, relationship building activities, and sports. I encourage learning the basics and taking it to a level that your dog finds challenging or interesting or rewarding. Some dogs do not enjoy academics. If they do, I will show you how to take it to the next level. If they don't, I like to introduce people and their dogs to sports.

For the purpose of puppies, we will start with the bare bone basics.

Place your dog in a sit.

Don't reward the sit.

Take one step back and return to your dog. Offer the treat. Say "good job!"

Next,

Repeat,

But, this time, take two steps back and return to your dog.

What do we say???   Good job!!!

Continue this exercise until you can get many steps across the room.

Take this exercise outdoors and then to other challenging places.

Smoothing out the Ruff Spots:

Dog won't stay.

Start with a prolonged sit. Then reward.

Advance to a prolonged sit and a simple lean back, and then lean forward, then reward.

This needs to be short and sweet in the beginning. Ask your pup to sit. Take one step back and return to him and reward!!!

Val is demonstrating a lean back with a prolonged sit.

This leads us to….

Mealtime Manners:

Please ask your dog to wait before bowling into their bowl.

Attempt to set the bowl of food onto the ground in front of your dog

but not too close. Chow hounds may be eager beavers to dive in.

And you have not rung the chow bell yet.

If they attempt to dive in,

raise the bowl and ask for a sit and attempt to place the bowl of food

on the ground again.

Usually, dogs will make several attempts to dive in before they

question what your motives are.

Repeat these efforts.

Once the dog is finally in a stay and not tackling the food bowl, set it

on the ground and release your dog to eat. Say "OK!"

Ask your pup to wait to eat. Hold onto the bowl. Don't let them eat

until you give the A OK.

Evo is demonstrating mealtime manners.

Smoothing out the Ruff Spots:

Dog gets to food before you release him = you are too slow :) Do not put food within reach.

Dog sits but dives into bowl as soon as it hits the ground = Keep your hand on the bowl and raise back up until you have released your pup.

Walk with me:

Walking with your dog is a fun, social, beneficial activity for both of you. When he is old enough and it is safe to do so. Besides the obvious exercise benefits, the social aspects are a tremendous asset as well. Start by walking around the house and have your dog follow you. Say "Here we go!" or "Lets walk!" You can even use a toy or a treat to lure him. Start to have him become familiar with the leash. Do the same exercise of having him follow you now attached to a lightweight leash. Do not pull on the leash. Keep the leash loose so that your dog learns that you won't pull him, and he won't pull you. Harnesses are the best tool to walk your pup with. Collars can pull on your dogs windpipe and cause trauma. It's best to pick a side you want your dog to walk on. Right or Left. If he stops… lure him and call him in happy voice to get him back on track. If he pulls you… you stop, and lure him back to your side. The biggest complication people have with walking their dog is pulling. Start young, start right, have fun with your dog while loose leash walking.

Doorway manners:

This is a lifesaving cue as well as an injury prevention cue. Teaching your pup doorway manners will reduce the risk of him getting injured by traffic, and or knocking you over while trying to bolt out the door. This is the polite and proper thing for pups to do.

Ask your pup to sit several feet away from the door.

Open the door a crack. If he gets up, close the door. Repeat this until he keeps his bottom on the ground through several door opening and closing sessions. Reward the desired response when he gives it to you.

Make sure your dog is securely leashed. Open the door and

keep your pup in a sit stay.

Then call them through and reward.

Come:

Come Rover! Yay!

Did you hear the excitement and enthusiasm in my voice? Initially

getting your dog to want to come to you might require a little enticement. The word 'COME', should represent good things are about to happen. You can motivate your pup with a treat to start, then an affectionate pat, a rub up, dinner, a walk, or a play session. Puppy ping-pong or round robin is a fun family interactive game to enhance recall skills. All family members start with a hand full of treats. You start in a small circle or just across from each other and each time you call his name, he will bound over to you to get the goody. After he gets his goodie from you, take one step back to increase the distance and the challenge. Calling your pup randomly for good things to happen, will pave the road to a solid recall when they are all grown up. When your pup comes to you, it should be rewarding and inviting.

Do not ever call your pup to come to you to scold him. This will make him think twice about coming the next time and put a damper on your recall. If the consequences of coming to you are unpleasant, the behavior will be avoided. (See Consequences).

Is your pup a Nose it all yet?

Lets do 2 more.

Leave it:

This is an impulse control exercise and also teaches them to leave things alone. This can also become a trick. You will soon be able to put a treat on your pups paw or nose while they sit there impressively!

Put a low value treat in your right hand and a high value reward treat in your left hand. Put your left hand with the reward behind your back. Hold your right hand closed, in front of your pups nose. Be patient. Don't move your hand. The second he leaves your hand alone, quickly reward from the left hand! Yay!

Evo ignoring or leaving my hand alone. Leave it.

Evo being rewarded with a higher value treat for

leaving it.

Photo: Nala demonstrating an excellent 'Leave It' cue on her second birthday.

Drop it:

Drop it is what you need when you are experiencing 'Leave It'

Failure. :)

If you have ever chased your pup to regain possession of an item...

Game on. This results in the need to teach a retrieve and a drop it

skill. Go get your self a high value goodie. Go get something for

your dog to trade with you. A ball or a toy. When your pup has the

toy in his mouth, put the treat in front of your dogs nose, and in a

nice voice, say "drop it." Do this repeatedly. If you have a retriever

type breed, you will soon notice them dropping things at your feet

and in your lap for the pleasant consequences that come with being a

good pup.

Bring it:

This is the combination of bringing it to you, and dropping it. This

starts with a good recall. If your pup has something you don't want

them to have, grab your goodie out of the close at hand goodie jar,

and lure them by showing them the treat. In your most attractive ice

cream voice, say, "Rover, bring it." When they do, trade the treat

and praise the dog.

A Release Word:

This is used to let your dog know they are 'all done' or they can be released from the cue. When they wait to eat, as in mealtime manners, you can say, "okay".

When they wait at the door and you are ready to release them from the wait you can say "Okay," "All Done," "Lets go," or "Finito!"

Inspirational:

The Benefits of Pet Companionship. Everywhere you turn, information on the benefits of pet companionship is abounding. You are probably gushing with happy hormones right now just being in the mere presence of your little bundle of yummy fur puppyness. Here is just a quickie list on the Dog gone good reasons for pet ownership.

The news, online articles, social media, and classes about the human animal bond focus on physical, emotional, therapeutic and social benefits of pet companionship. Here are some wonderfully pawsative reasons to have a dog in your life.

Dogs promote happiness through a release of happy hormones such as oxytocin and serontonin. They are a four-legged anti-depressant.

Dogs need and promote exercise. You always have and exercise partner.

Dogs are Date magnets. For you single people, your dog could introduce you to the person of your dreams. Like in 101 Dalmations! Therapy dogs have been assisting people in many ways for many years. We can now add Post Traumatic Stress Relief therapy dogs, as well as Diabetic dogs,

Seizure dogs, and Cancer detecting dogs to that list. The biggest recent role dogs have on the health industry is with autistic children. In the presence of dogs, children with autism can come out of their shell, improve communication, and reduce other unwanted behaviors.

Dogs have been reported to lower blood pressure and it is stated the prognosis for surviving a heart condition is better if you have a dog in your life.

Socialization is a perk to having a dog. People enjoy engaging with other dog loving individuals. Dog parties and dog friendly social events are a fun way to interact with others.

Dogs can reduce allergens in some children. On the aspect of children, dogs teach children responsibility and how to be caring and empathetic.

I know what you're thinking. You'll take two!

Canine Comedy and near the Tail End of the Book:

Fun sayings and quotes.

OCD = Obsessive Canine Disorder

I like big mutts and I cannot lie

I love my wiener

I kissed a dog and liked it

Dogs have owners, cats have staff

You had me at woof

In dog years I'm dead

Be the person your dog thinks you are

Life is short, play with your dog

No outfit is complete without dog hair

Dog hair, it's a condiment

To err is human, to forgive is canine

In dog beers, I've only had one

My windows aren't dirty, that's dog nose art

Dogs are not our whole lives, but they make are lives whole

Dogs welcome, people tolerated

All you need is love and a dog

I'm not perfect, but my dog thinks I'm awesome

I want to be the person my dog thinks I am

My kids drink out of the toilet

Have you hugged your dog today

Get your Basset moving

My Labrador retriever is smarter then your honor student

Every day is hump day in this house

Husband and Labrador missing. Reward for Lab

If my dog doesn't like you, I probably don't either

I sleep with dogs

References

I would like to give credit to several books and multiple websites

that I referenced during the information gathering process of this

book. I did not cite anyone or any references in this book. I merely

utilized these resources to confirm my affirmations, knowledge, and

to reassure myself I did not leave any dog diggin important

information out of this book.

www.apdt.com. The American Pet Dog Trainer Association

Organization and website. This is a professional organization I have

belonged to for about 10 years. They provide a wealth of information

on a humane and P+ levels.

www.aspca.org. ASPCA. The American Society for the Protection

of Cruelty to Animals, website. This site actually offers a good

amount of P+ and behavioral information for everything from basic

manners to behavioral problems and then some.

NA. (2006). Maran Illustrated Puppies. This is a thorough and P+ book with lots of good descriptive pictures.

Miller, Pat. (2001). The Power of Positive Dog Training. My first and most impressionable dog book that I have had the pleasure of reading. This book made most sense to me as I was breaking into the world of dog training. I still buy this book on line for students and employees. Pat Miller is probably the only person I have been star struck by.

O'Heare, J. (2007). Aggressive Behavior in Dogs. This was my reference for the developmental stages of dogs.

Important Digits

(You will need to dial since your dog does not have a thumb).

Dog Trainers

Name_____
_

Number_____Email_____

Veterinarians

Name_____
_

Number_____Email_____

Emergency
Vet_____

Number_____
_

Pet Sitter

Name_____
_

Number_____Email_____

Doggie Daycare/Hotel/

Name_____
_

Number_____
_

Groomer

Name_____Number_____

–

Name_____

–

Number_____

–

Notes_____

_____

_____

_____

_____

_____

_____

_____

This is my Send Rover on Over Mascot Doggie, drawn by
my friend Susan.

Made in the USA
San Bernardino, CA
29 July 2018